+LEADS

Simple Strategies That Work to Get Real Estate Leads Fast

JAMES HARRISON

TABLE OF CONTENTS

INTRODUCTION

Leads are the lifeblood of any sales career- Especially in Real Estate.

Being an agent is like running your own business. As you know, real estate brokers and agents depend on their sales, and earning that commission is crucial.

It's simple: more leads **always** mean more sales; and, of course, more business. This is where your success comes from. Being a great closer isn't everything. You could be the best salesman in the world- but still go broke, if you have no leads!

So- are you focusing on getting more leads in?

Of course, we all want an endless pipeline of fresh, hot-off-the-press leads, to help us get more reliable income and bring our business to new heights. When you start, it's not always so simple, and it can feel like it's just 'down to luck'.

This is a common- and serious- problem for:

- Real estate agents in an unfamiliar area, lacking connections
- New realtors who haven't yet learned the best ways to get leads
- People who finished school, and are interested in sales, but unsure how to take those early steps
- Real estate agents who really know what they're doing... But, hit a wall for no apparent reason, and have an empty, bone-dry lead pipeline

No matter what stage you're at... Lack of leads will ultimately cut down your career in real estate.

Finding qualified leads is hard and consumes lots of time and energy. Time that you should be able to spend on developing yourself or with loved ones.

Finally, we come to the crux of the issue:

How can you quickly land hot leads to get business (and income) to start flowing, without sacrificing all your personal time?

Here's where we get to the good news!

Unlike them, you're taking steps, in advance, to prevent this from happening. That's why you're reading this... And that's why I know you can make it.

From my own success in real estate, I can promise you this-

'Making it' in real estate sales is NOT magic, and it's NOT luck. It's about knowledge, intuition, and securing a solid ROI for your time and effort.

I've sold over 250 properties in my decade of realtor work. The beginning is the hardest part. I was barely keeping my head above water for the first 6 months.

One day, I realized I needed to learn, understand, and replicate the exact strategies used by the top performing agents.

I decided to simply analyse the top realtors, and learn all the little nuances of how they found leads, without driving themselves crazy with time and effort. I took all their secret strategies and tactics for myself and used them for my career.

This required about 2 years of intensely researching, and studying, my competitors. The work was brutal, but the payoff was worth it...

By the time I'd finished, my income had shot up 50%, while my overall workload actually *decreased*!

How's that possible?

It's simple, actually- this new series of strategies enabled me to:

- Only generate qualified, interested, warm leads, who won't waste your time and energy
- Free up more time to focus on brand and marketing
- Find leads who were already interested in my specific brand

That means more leads, with less work!

I'm no sales wizard- I just used the lead generation tactics that WORK.

If I could do it, I know you can.

Whether you're a brand new agent, or an experienced one who wants to get more business, I KNOW these tactics can help you.

Real estate is one of the most incredible, exciting opportunities for making money today- with unlimited earning potential, your ability to grow and thrive is totally up to you.

Curious to learn more, and take your lead generation to new heights?

Read on!

PART 1

Mindset, Database and Contact Plan

Generating a massive pipeline of leads comes down to your mindset, the system in place, database, and a contact plan.

Preparation is always necessary to ensure success. The truth is that there are 1.4 million licensed agents in the United States (US), according to data from The National Association of Agents (NAR) in 2019 (Rudden, 2020). Not surprisingly, this figure lets us know that unless we do the unthinkable, we will simply fade into the masses. However, there are many ways to make the difference, if you follow the techniques outlined in this guide, and mentally prepare yourself for the challenge.

The other truth that plays in our favor: 139.64 million residential properties recorded in 2019 (Rudden, 2020). This simply means that opportunities are everywhere. Also, gone are the days where properties stayed within a family for five generations. Understand the world, including properties and people, are in constant motion.

As long as an agent fully grasps the fundamentals, and minimum requirements needed to generate leads, they can stick their hands in an endless pot of gold. Keep in mind, you'll face challenges, but that's why I'm going to share with you all the most effective techniques to generate leads fast.

Win The Inner Game

Many expert brokers, including Tyler Zey from the Easy Agent Pro website, agree that we can't jump head-first into lead generation without the right attitude and a detailed plan (Zey, n.d.).

Your success in real estate will depend on your ability to choose and commit to an approach that works consistently. Remember, successful brokers, do just a few things, exceptionally well.

You need to always begin with the end in mind. The first part of planning your next move is determining who <u>you</u> want to be as an agent.

You can't find the answer to that, unless you know why you've chosen real estate. Once you know precisely <u>why</u> you're in this career, then everything will align and make sense. It will also save you years of struggle.

From a personal experience, "Motivation" is not the most important thing.

What really matters is the <u>reasons </u>why you do things, that's something that only you can uncover. Here are 3 simple questions to open space for thinking, generate more clarity, and reveal your aspirations:

- Think about the moment where you seriously thought about becoming successful in real estate. What got you exited in the first place? What did you see? What did you hear? What did you feel?
- Who do you admire the most in real estate? What is it about them that you want specifically? Why?

- Let's talk about conviction here. As you put ALL your doubts on the side now, what is <u>certain </u>about the person that you want to become in real estate? What is not negotiable? Why?

These 3 sharp questions will give you insights into what's needed next.

These are your motivators because no one can succeed in life without purpose.

You should feel a burning desire to move forward daily, and crush your goals. Motivation without purpose will get you nowhere. The truth is that careers have a deeper meaning, and that's what you must attach yourself to. As you face challenges, consistently working on generating leads, I'd suggest to naturally come back to those reasons.

Targeted Database For Growth

Agents can get leads from various sources. Every agent wants to grow a database, but the quality of our potential leads matters more than anything. There are 12 categories of lead sources. Each category can teach you how to prospect for the right kind of contacts.

Referrals

Referral leads are the eagle that soars above the rest. People tend to be influenced by a trusted friend before they'll consider ratings on a Facebook page. Referrals could be hard to come by for new agents. As you go about the strategies outlined in the next chapters, you'll notice a handful of different techniques to simply make this process easy for you.

Every agent should work on gaining trust and going above and beyond to start the referral generation engine. Giving clients an unforgettable experience is where you begin. You can also join referral sources such as Referral Exchange, Agent Hero, and Opacity to start.

Organic

Organic leads can be another gem for you once you're up and running. You don't find these contacts, but they find you because you put yourself in a position to be found. This is often achieved by having a search engine optimization (SEO) page catered for lead magnets on your website, and SEO optimized articles to bring your page to the top of search engine results pages (SERPs).

Organic leads are anyone you gain as a contact without effort or financial commitment. Your followers on Facebook, YouTube channel subscribers, and regular blog subscribers are all organic audiences. They make a great target because they come to your door.

Portals

Portal leads are the ones you get from Zillow, Homes.com, and Realtor.com. Any leads generated through these portals are high-profile contacts because they're specifically in the market to buy or sell a home. All you have to do is be the fastest responding agent as many portal websites link multiple agents to one listing. These leads are like hot potatoes waiting for the first agent to manage them.

Pay-Per-Click (PPC)

Google AdWords and BoomTown are perfect examples of PPC lead generation. This is a powerful way for skilled marketing gurus to strike gold. Ad copy testing, conversion rates, and optimization on these platforms can be hair-raising and highly competitive. It's possible to do this yourself, but I recommend outsourcing your PPC marketing campaign to professionals like social media agency.

The other deterrent for new agents is that genuine leads through PPC can become pricey. Many top brokers rely heavily on PPC marketing, but the competitive edge combined with the cost per lead can be overwhelming if you have a small budget.

Social Media

Social media leads can be run as paid, or you can target organic reach. Both options have pros and cons. The reason why social media leads can become costly is that they rely on using algorithms to target demographic groups. Some of the people who see your ads won't even be interested in a property. However, social media lead generation is far cheaper than AdWords and can be an excellent source for new agents who have the time to sort genuine contacts from people.

Lists

SmartZip, RedX, and LandVoice can help you build lists where you're trying to establish new relationships. These programs can help you target for sale by owner (FSBO) or expired listings, among others, and build a database on that.

Motivated Seller Leads

This is another gold mine opportunity. Motivated sellers are ready to sell. This could be because they're starting a new job somewhere, are in foreclosure, or going through a separation. These leads can be attracted by canvassing the neighborhood with yard signs and running ad campaigns to make sure they know your name.

Cash Buyers

Who doesn't love the smell of crisp notes? Cash buyers are another category on their own, but they can be hard to come by. Agents who don't want to wait weeks for financial assistance to be approved can focus on cash buyers. Some databases can put you in contact with these gems, such as Zillow.

Private Lender Leads

Many people don't trust banks and large institutions anymore, especially after the 2008 stock market crash. The good thing is that you could benefit from contacting a few private lenders who can share with you qualified leads.

Direct Mail Leads

Many agents, especially on a low budget, still use the valuable trick of blanketing an entire neighborhood in postcards and direct mail drop-offs. You can stand out by walking up to the door and greeting the person instead of dropping it in their mailbox. Besides, personal introductions automatically set the tone.

Probate Leads

Probate leads are an underestimated type of lead, because finding them can be difficult at first. Honestly, many properties enter the legal status of inherited property more than often. It can be daunting to deal with emotional families, but agents can turn these into long-term relationships.

Partner Leads

Partner leads are another great source of genuine contact. These are the leads you gain through partnering with other businesses in your area. No business is untouchable, and that makes this a great strategy. You could partner with restaurants who see hundreds of faces every month, hardware stores where people buy building material, and you can even sponsor a local sports team in return for wearing your brand.

There's an endless source of possibilities for targeting the right category to quickly get your pipeline full and your business booming.

A Robust Contact Plan With An Automated Follow-Up System

Let's face it, trying to generate leads without a plan in place is like hopping into the fast lane with a bicycle, and no helmet.

The contact plan will decide how you interact with your database.

A contact plan is the next part of your success preparation. It's the system you use to stay in touch with your database over time, or build new relationships. Another interesting agent term, a client touchpoint, describes the interaction you have with a contact. This could be emails, holiday greetings, text messages, or invitations to events.

We can also learn more about customer relationship management (CRM), which can facilitate your life and skyrocket your pipeline by orders of magnitude. CRM managers are websites that handle all the client touchpoints in your contact plan for you. They manage relationships and interactions with customers or potential leads.

Having a CRM set up correctly could ease the process for you. It smooths your organization so that you don't miss specific milestones in contacting your database, planning, and managing your time and leads automatically. These automated managers ease the accountability, and effort required for an effective contact plan.

Let's look at software automation you can use from the simplest to the most advanced ones that require some experience.

Freshsales is the first on our list. This platform is user friendly for new agents, but it depends on your ability to bring leads into your database. Once you have contacts, you have a fully automated and simple-to-use software to manage and connect with them.

HubSpot CRM is one of the more popular choices for newer agents because it's free. This software takes minutes to learn, and allows you to organize, set reminders, and manage your client touchpoints with ease.

Zillow Premier Agent is another good choice. Zillow allows their agents to use insights unfound anywhere else. You can see your client's history and make contact at appropriate times based on their activity. This platform also allows you to deepen your relationship by removing other agents from a contact's viewed listings after the initial connection.

Agile CRM comes in fourth place. This platform has various options, from novice to advanced. New agents could use it to manage their database and generate leads on a free version for up to 10 users. Seasoned agents could use this platform for advanced analytics and marketing campaign management.

Finally, **Bitrix24** has a spot as well. This automation platform is excellent for seasoned agents as it offers a variety of workflow processes, including CRM. The only issue is all the options available, and that can be overwhelming for a new agent.

Maybe you are just starting, and you want to speed up the process. Well, the easiest and most accessible way to build your database for future contact plans without a CRM is to design a spreadsheet in Google Docs. This allows you to manage your client touchpoints manually until you have an automated system (which I highly recommend). It's also easy to export the information into a software platform later on.

You want to create columns on the left. Your labels for columns should include name, last name, company name, title, phone number, mobile number, email address, physical address, where you met, birthdays, previous business transactions, social media accounts, and interests from a survey you might've conducted. <u>The more information you have in each column, the better your communication will be.</u>

You can also use different tabs at the bottom of the spreadsheet to sort your contact list into various lead categories. All you need to do is fill the columns up with information from contacts you meet. Agents who don't want to rely solely on their CRMs can do this one thing, and generates new leads.

Additionally any agent needs a website with a blog. *84% of successful agents use blog content articles on their websites to generate qualified leads (Zey, n.d.). This also means that they interact with their contacts weekly, without fail.*

Here's another important thing to keep in mind before we move along, even a past buyer or seller remains a contact. You have a high chance of doing repeat business with someone who interacted with you before.

The key is to be <u>systematic</u> in contacting all individuals in your database. Setting A daily routine can mean the difference between getting what you want or feeling helpless. The money will follow as long as you spend allocated time every morning with your client touchpoints.

Lead generation through interacting with your database is the first thing you do every morning when you arrive. You must become hyper intentional in your communication.

Now we can move on to the crucial stage of planning your contact touchpoints. There are multiple ways to do this.

The 8x8 Magic Introduction

This technique is best used for new customers who you're forming a relationship with. The basic principle of this is to make meaningful contact with new prospects and clients weekly for 8 weeks. You don't want to call them every week, so let's look at an example of what you can do.

Week 1: Send an introduction email, text message, or give them a call. There is one key point here. Always add value. Especially at the beginning of the interaction. Ask them if there's anything you can help them with.

Week 2: You can send them an interesting fact or an informative video.

Week 3: Connect to your prospect on social media. I know this might sound pushy, but it's necessary. If you already have them on one platform, add them to another. Also, go on to their page and comment or like a post.

Week 4: Send them an email with a market-related interest, such as the trend in property values at the time.

Week 5: You can send them another text or call them. Check in with them to see if they have any questions for you.

Week 6: Make your prospect feel appreciated with a personal gift or a handwritten note. Handwritten notes are underestimated in business. It shows a personal interest in the prospect.

Week 7: Send your future client another informative snippet. You can invite them to your blog posts or share a news article.

Week 8: Call or send a video message to reassure your prospect that you're here if they need any information. You can invite them for a video chat on Zoom or Skype.

Personal Contact

This takes us back to the beginning. The best way to build a lasting and meaningful relationship is to make personal contact on occasion. People love seeing the face behind a name and would appreciate bumping into you and chatting. Don't hide from any customers, even if you're out of the office today. Walk up to any contact and greet them with a firm handshake.

Stay Top of Mind Strategy

This one is for closing sales and aftercare. Don't forget the customers who trusted you after you cash the check. Keep them in the loop with monthly emails covering local market news. After all, this contact is new to the area. Add a quarterly mail where you invite them to events where they can meet the community. You can top this off with a comparative market analysis (CMA) twice a year.

What are the most critical touchpoints?

1. Forms submission
2. Phone calls
3. Text messages
4. In-person visits
5. Emails

If you want to increase your touchpoints' impact, *quantity and speed* are your two most important assets. Especially for your online leads, speed is vital. The longer you wait and the less chance you have for them to follow up.

That's why it's vital for real estate agents to receive instant notifications from identifying hot leads.

*Having a follow-up system in place that is relevant and automated **is** the secret to exceptionally increase your client portfolio by orders of magnitude.*

Powerful Automated System

I'm sharing with you bellow the follow-up system that literally double my sales in just a few months. It's easy and can be implemented by new agents. The most important thing I want you to understand is this:

This is what I call a <u>CLEAR PROCESS TO REVENUE.</u>

Ad + Quiz + Automated Follow up = $!

If you want direct results, this is the **formula** I use to get a constant stream of leads and business.

Here is how you are going to implement this strategy:

Step 1: Create a Quiz with bucket.io

Step 2: Create a simple Facebook ad to promote the Quiz

Step 3: Set up the automatic follow up system with "Howde" or another software.

Step 4: Link the Quiz form to the follow-up system (howde) with Zapier

<u>Step 1: The Quiz</u>

Quiz is the number one most powerful way to get qualified and motivated leads fighting for your attention.

Here is how the automation works:

The concept is simple: Start from a Facebook ad to promote a quiz, and follow up on qualified leads with automatic text, email, and voicemail.

So once the leads start coming in, there's not much else to do. You just let the system follow up naturally. It works really well.

Each question in the Quiz has a specific purpose. Not only the Quiz qualify the leads more, because it takes more work to go through the questions and enter their information to talk to you, but also pre-frame them in such a way that you become the prize.

Here are a few examples of questions you can use to design your Quiz:

"Do you currently rent or own?"

That's an important question for a real estate agent because, for example, this is a home buyer campaign, and renting or owning a home can lead to a different conversation. In this campaign, we are interested in people currently renting a home and looking for buying one.

- Rent?
- Own?

"Where are you looking to purchase?"

So when you contact them, you now know exactly where they're looking to buy their next piece of real estate.

- Enter location

"When are you planning to request your Home Loan Benefits?

- Within a month
- 2-5 months
- In more than 5 months
- Unsure

This is telling you when they're looking to get a Home Loan. Now you can talk to your mortgage loan officer and say, " Hey, I have a person looking to get a loan in 2-5 months.."

" What's your price range ?" (An estimate is fine)

- $100,000 – $200,000
- $200,000 – $300,000
- $300,000 – $400,000
- $400,000 or more

This tells you what type of house they're looking for.

"What is your estimated credit score?" (Just a guess is fine)

- Below fair (580 -619)
- Fair (620 – 659)
- Good (660 – 739)
- Great (740+)

This is important to know when it comes to buying a home because if it's below fair more than likely, they're not going to qualify to get a home loan.

Now that you have the mindset, the database and the contact plan ready and a follow-up system, it's time to move on to strategies.

"How much would you like to borrow? (Just an estimate...)

- $100,000 – $200,000
- $200,001 – $300,000
- $300,001 – $400,000
- more than $400,000

All these are questions that can be used when you follow up with the lead, and you can also use them when you're talking with a mortgage loan officer to get people pre-approved for a home loan.

"Have you ever purchased a home?"

- Yes
- No

It's a different conversation. If somebody has bought a home before they have different questions. For first time buyers, it's an entirely different story.

"Are you currently employed?"

- Yes
- No

That tells if they can qualify for a home loan.

"Are you currently working with a realtor ?"

- Yes
- No

If they are already working with somebody, they are no need to work with them. We can keep them in the database, but that's about it.

For different campaigns, when you are creating your questions, think about what's relative to your client and what information will be important for you to move on.

Step 2: The Facebook Ad

Create or have someone to create a Facebook ad promoting your Quiz.

For example, we can target first time home buyers with a title like :

"Take this 9 question quiz to find out if you're ready to buy a home in the Nashville area. (link to quiz landing page)"

- Create a Facebook community page for your targeted area.
- Set up the ad on Facebook and Instagram news feed.
- Optimize your campaign for landing page views.

Your lead can now click on the link and access the quiz landing page.

Now their information is sent over to your automated system follow up system, called "Howde".

Step 3: The Follow-up System

With Howde, you can set the automation this way:

- Within the first 5 minutes, you can send them out a pre-recorded voicemail. (you can set up the follow up whenever you want)
- In the next 7 minutes, they receive a text message
- Then an email is sent out 15 minutes after the Quiz is completed

When you set up your Turbo campaign on Howde, you basically need 3 lists :

- General List (For new leads coming in)
- Responded List (if they respond)
- Not Responded List (if they don't respond)

This automated system automatically allows you to follow up with all your most qualified and motivated leads as quickly as possible. You can set up a 10 day follow up like the following:

DAY 1

- Voicemail
- Text SMS
- Email

DAY 2

- Text SMS

DAY 3

- Voicemail
- Email
- Text SMS

DAY 4

- Text SMS

DAY 5

- Text SMS
- Email

DAY 6

- Voicemail

DAY 7

- Text SMS
- Email

DAY 10

- Email

This formula is great because, on average, it takes 7 to 15 touches/follow-ups to get someone to respond.

This is for example, a 14-touch system that is completely hands-free and automated. **All you have to do is wait for people to respond.** You can even have a follow-up system up to a FULL year. That's really powerful for your leads.

When the leads respond, they will be taken out of the automation, and that's the beauty of this automated follow-up system, so you can pick up the conversation as if it were anyone else reaching out to them.

The goal of this follow up system is to look natural. You can edit the text, email that goes out, and record your voicemail.

For the Quiz, I suggest using "Bucket.io" to create different segmentation and provide different questions depending on their answers. For example, one of the most important questions could be, "What is your credit score?" that's probably one of the most important questions. You can set up 2 thank you pages : Good credit, thank you page, and Bad credit thank you page. We only want to track good credit leads.

Simply set up the questions, design, Facebook pixel (if you have one), then publish it.

Step 4: Connect them all with Zapier.

Now let's move to Zapier to connect and automate the follow-up system and the Quiz.

- Create a simple Zap between your Quiz (bucket.io) and your follow up (Howde). That's going to create the action of adding that new contact into Howde.
- You can also create another quick Zap (Send Outbound email) to notify you by email as soon as a new lead comes in.

You now have a simple revenue-generating system.

However, I need to tell you, there is a cost to run this system, and it's going to be about ~200$/month in total. Keep in mind, It's well-invested money because it will come back tenfold, giving you peace of mind knowing that you have a pipeline full of opportunity, and making your life easier.

Now that you have the mindset, the database, the contact plan ready, and follow up system. It's time to move on to strategies.

PART 2:

Lead Generation Strategies

Now let's talk about lead generation strategies. You must find the turbo booster that can help you enter the fast lane without being crushed by the agents who are cruising comfortably. These proven lead generation techniques are simple enough to implement for new agents to quickly get them started on building a full pipeline. These strategies can be implemented immediately and effectively; however, you'll need to put effort in.

This section is filled with multiple strategies to generate leads and ways to follow up with people. You need to know that not every strategy works for every agent, but the idea is to test and learn which methods work best for you, while constantly recalibrating your strategy. Some prospects prefer strict business relationships where others will love the personal relationship built over time.

The most successful agents agree that a combination of strategies is needed to succeed. <u>The more contact points you have with a client, the better</u>. Your contact plan will be tested and readjusted as you learn to know which interactions work for you. Follow-ups should be done through multiple channels for the best results.

CHAPTER 1:

Sphere of Influence Leads

New agents must start with the most efficient lead generation engine they can design from day one.

Your sphere of influence (SOI) represents a massive chunk of your future clients and must be prioritized above all other strategies. This valuable technique isn't optional if you want to succeed in real estate. That's why you must get started with this plan immediately.

Robert Rico, a real estate guru, explains that having a functional SOI is like adding gas to the fire of your success (CA Realty aiming, 2017). You might as well start shoveling the driveway during a blizzard if you dismiss this strategy. The benefits of having an SOI are endless. These people know you and respect your opinion. Besides, no additional effort is needed to interact with people who you already have relationships with.

More than half of millennial buyers—the market boomers of today—have purchased a home through a referral from a friend or relative, according to NAR (Simmons, 2020). This proves how we can use our SOI to build a solid referral network. Another report from the NAR shows that 90% of buyers would use the same agent again (Simmons, 2019). This means that we can use our SOI contacts as silent salespeople.

Where do you start? Your SOI begins with people in your personal and professional network with whom your opinion holds some weight. This network doesn't contain people who you've never met. These SOIs can be designed among various people you know, and those you're going to introduce yourself to. Your automatic referral team will grow with time.

An example of an agent's personal SOI would include family, friends, parents, and friends by relative association. It can also include your coworkers if you have a close relationship with them and long-standing social media contacts.

An example of an agent's professional SOI would include professional organizations, coworkers, and businesses. You could establish relationships with vendors, property managers, mortgage brokers, insurance companies, personal bankers, commercial lenders, bakeries, landscapers, cleaning services, staging experts, title companies, property developers, investors, and out of state agents for referrals.

The only question you want to focus on is... who do you know? Start your list today, and work on growing it steadily. Let's see what successful brokers do to increase their SOI.

Build a Team of Silent Salespeople

David Rusenko once said, *"Word of mouth is a crucial component of organic growth for start-ups."*

Your real estate career is a start-up as it's a battlefield of entrepreneurship. It's a fact proven by the survey results we saw from NAR. It's easier to approach a friend for advice than to walk up to an agent who doubles as a stranger.

Selling or buying a home is a major development in someone's life, and they're more comfortable chatting to someone in a relaxed setting, such as barbeques, parties, or even over the watercooler at work. These non-intrusive scenarios turn a business chat into friendly banter. So, when you have "silent salespeople" among friends and family, they'll interrupt someone who talks about buying a home.

This person steps in and says, "I know a guy" without you batting an eyelid. The person they interrupt will also take your contact details because they have some social connection to the natural sphere of influence with the silent salesperson. This is the immediate silent salespeople you want on your team.

<u>The key that most agents forgot is to add each person in your personal contacts to your contact plan to remind them of your work so that they can sell for you.</u>

More often than not, new agents will just assume their silent sales team is "promoting" them, but relationships are dynamics things. You must remind your team and keep sharing your progress with them.

Taking Action

1. Commit to growing your social group.
2. Find one event or activity weekly where you can socialize and meet new salespeople.

3. Chat to a minimum of three new people by asking them about themselves as one would do in regular small talk.
4. Remember that this isn't a sales pitch, but it's only the establishment of new connections.
5. Use subtle methods of bringing your line of work or current real estate news into the conversation.
6. Invite one new connection to attend another event.
7. Keep your team updated on your progress.

This is how we build friendships, and you can be assured that you'll leave a lasting impact as long as you don't make these interactions sound like sales pitches.

Forming Business Alliances

This is a straightforward strategy to implement yet remarkably effective.

You can form an affiliate connection with many businesses to make sure your business card is in the hands of anyone who could recommend you.

If you have a loyal insurance broker in your business alliance, who sends leads your way while, whenever you have the opportunity, suggest that broker to your clients. You must return the favor.

New agents might not have any relationships with business owners in their area. That doesn't mean you can't have this mutual relationship.

The secret here is to Look for the obvious bridge between real estate and other businesses.

We can focus on prospecting for leads through insurance companies, personal bankers, commercial lenders, title companies, property management specialists, and landscapers famous for turning heads with his projects.

As soon as you introduce yourself to these people and work on forming a deeper connection, you can be assured of obtaining an omnipresence where you get loads of referrals.

You can achieve this by calling a company and inviting the landscaper to meet over lunch. You can also reach out to affiliates by offering them incentives for referring business your way, and ask how you can do the same for them.

Taking Action

1. Find sales representatives who provided services to other businesses in the area on LinkedIn and Facebook.
2. Meet in a coffee shop where business is more casual and personal.
3. Ask your potential affiliate about their best-selling product or service. **Always give Value first.** Think first : "What can I do for them?" " How can I help them?" "Who can I connect with them?"
4. Tell them about yourself and your real estate values in an elevator-style sales pitch.
5. Finally, ask if they'd like to partner with you and offer them a referral commission for referrals that close a sale.

All you want to do after this is to develop the relationship that needs a perfect blend of friendly connections and business-related touchpoints.

Collaboration with Coworkers

Real estate is truly one of the most competitive careers. New agents come on board, and the first thing they want to do is topple their seniors. Let's face it; a real estate company is commonly seen as a collection of individual entrepreneurs battling it out. That's where ideas are misunderstood, and new agents fall.

Realty is an individual sport if I can call it that, but you can't walk into an office and see your coworkers as enemies. Yes, one day, you wish to outsell them. You want to topple the hierarchy of value as being the irreplaceable person on the team. However, you're not going to do this by overthrowing the leaders in your agency overnight.

You must learn to work with your coworkers and build solid relationships where you can depend on each other. Think of it as finding a mentor at work. Focus on the agent who handles high-end, million-dollar listings in your agency. Not only can you learn from them, but you can build a tag team that will be needed from both of you when you become successful too.

You won't be able to handle all your leads and follow-ups alone, and neither can a busy, successful realtor. Agents who work collaboratively with each other can send referrals to other agents.

Taking Action

Choose a mentor and work on building a tag team with them.

1. Set your sights on the most successful agent in your company.
2. Offer them lunch to speak to them about your career.
3. Tell this person that you wish to learn from them in a mentoring partnership.
4. Ask if there's anything you can help them with, which will provide learning opportunities for you. This could be handling their leads.
5. Ask your mentor if you can accompany them to open houses and meet new clients.

Most agents feel proud that you chose them, and the more time you spend together, the stronger your tag team partnership becomes.

Agent Tours

Your SOI shouldn't be limited to your office, either. Some of you might also work alone after just receiving your license, and need some backup from other private agents.

Tag team efforts are one way of thinking about networking, but we can also think of it as keeping your friends close and your competition closer.

Harsh intentions with networking aren't always fruitful though. The benefits of meeting and connecting with other agents are to pick up the tricks of the trade, gain referrals for your specific niche, learn about conferences and events in the area, and create that tag-team effort with someone who might turn out to be a valuable partner.

Where can you meet these people without walking into their office? Local caravans and agent tours are the best way we can network with other agents. Many agents think of these events as hard work, and others believe these will lead to closing a sale, but this is rarely true.

The most significant benefit of these events is that we can prospect and build a referral network. Many caravans are hosted by top local brokers looking for someone to take on a listing that you're visiting in the open house caravan. This could also work in your favor, especially when you become a regular, and the brokers notice this.

Taking Action

Commit to a networking plan that boosts your influence in the local industry.

1. Set two calendar reminders of local caravans or agent tours to attend monthly.
2. Aim at connecting with three agents at each event.
3. Make it your mission to strike up a short conversation with the host broker.
4. Hand them your business card.
5. Continue showing up regularly and chatting to the host each time. This starts imprinting your face in their minds.
6. You can start personalizing your small talk after the third visit. Ask the broker about their kids and what they thought of Saturday night's game.

Pro Tip: You might get a listing that another agent turned down, and I'm sure you'll be more than happy to share a referral commission from a listing you wouldn't have had if you didn't attend the tour.

Out of Town Referral Network

Jennie Wolek, a high-profile agent who sells 100 homes a year, has one more trick to put up your sleeve (Icenhower Coaching, 2016). "Out of town" referral networks are a deep well of referral potential. This is the next step in broadening your SOI with more agents that aren't necessarily in your locality.

This strategy is often overlooked because it requires a bit of persistence; that's why it's so powerful. However, what happens to that property when a potential affiliate agent sells a client's home two states over, and now, they want to sell their home in your state? This is common with high-end clients who own multiple properties around the country.

What if that agent had your business card, and remembered the personality behind the conversation you had at the conference a few months back? They could recommend you to their existing client who is part of their SOI now, and all you'd have to do is pay them a referral fee.

You can also send them a handwritten thank you card with a bottle of champagne when the sale closes. Agents should start working on their out of town or state referral networks as early as they can. You could even have another agent refer someone who wants to buy a house in your town after selling one in theirs. The possibilities are endless.

Taking Action

Before I begin, make sure your business cards have addresses and zip codes on them so that they don't get tossed in the trash by agents who forget where you're based as soon as they leave the event.

1. Find two out of state, or out of town events you can attend annually.
2. Take those informative business cards along.
3. Introduce yourself to seven agents. Don't just hand them your card and say thanks. You should strike up an engaging conversation because this is another relationship you're building.
4. Practice one quote, joke, or memorable thing to say for each encounter.
5. Collect as many business cards as you hand out. Remember that all relationships are two-way streets. You could also earn referral fees.

Your primary goal in this is to make your meeting memorable. Once you have their card, you can continue with your systematic touchpoints to keep yourself fresh in their minds.

Investor Networks

The investor network is often seen as a complex, yet it is an effective strategy to generate leads. The problem is that most people who aren't desperate to sell their properties are looking to get the full retail value of it, whereas investors are looking to profit. That makes you the middleman in a negotiation. Both parties are of interest to you, so how do you solve this problem? Embrace the middleman position!

Investor networks are a massive addition to your database. You can design your own seller leads strategy through investors. Keep in mind that not every investor is a real estate guru. That's the skills you offer them along with some incentives. The fact that these people aren't real estate giants means that they can't capitalize on any leads.

Investors are business-minded individuals, and as long as it's a give and take relationship, you're good to go. They can send leads your way, and you can help them turn a profit on properties where both of you win.

Taking Action

New agents have this misunderstanding that investors are people with flashy cars and skyscrapers in New York. However, the secret is that everyone is an investor. Anyone who has a business mind, profits in their sights, and some money to spend is an investor. In this exercise, you're going to focus on growing and maintaining investors from easily accessible sources. Aim at having 10 investors you can connect with monthly.

1. Auctions are an excellent place to scoop investors because they're bargain hunting and in the right mindset from the word *sold*.
2. Social media is another way of generating investor leads through groups.
3. Home expos and trade shows are where you can find home improvers who double as investors.
4. Attend Real Estate Investor Association and Landlord Association meetings to make a few connections.
5. Chamber of Commerce groups and events can also be a catalyst for meeting investors in the line of attorneys, accountants, and bankers.

All you have to do is keep your eye on the ball of gaining enough investor contacts to connect within your contact plan. As an incentive, many agents pay their investors attractive referral fees and vice versa. There's also generally a quick turnover of settlements. The bonus comes when you get to manage any property you sell to an investor, growing your asset base.

Friends with Developers

Property developers and builders shouldn't just become your friends. You should become their preferred agent who has as much desire to move their stock as fast as possible. The more property they have sitting in the unsold bin, the more costly it is, and they can see narrowed profit margins.

Developers and builders are usually involved with massive projects that could provide agents with years of sales potential. You can also manage these developments once they're in place. The biggest battle for new agents is to get their foot in the door. So, how do you meet these industry giants?

Developers and builders are a vast market, and your best bet is to search for local faces. You can include a few towns close by if you're willing to travel. Next, you set up a meeting with them. Most big developers will be busy and will annoyingly reschedule your meeting. This is when you become a little pushier. You're in sales, after all. You can also "bump into them" casually or meet them at conferences, events, and development associations.

Taking Action

Once you get your foot in the door, remember that this relationship is for the long haul. You need to gain their trust, and you must offer them something other agents haven't. You can combine the two as a promise to show them what you're made of. Let's see what this meeting should entail.

1. You must have a good idea about their development or construction business from the research you did before your arrival.
2. Pinpoint any similarities you have in values.
3. Compliment them on an achievement you noticed in your research. This makes the meeting more personal and admirable.
4. Ask them about what they wish to achieve in the short term.
5. Tell them about any previous partnerships you might've had that were successful.
6. Make them an offer they can't refuse, even if this means you must knock your commission down to ensure a deal.

Long-term relationships such as this one could yield progressive results rather than a get rich quick approach. The longer you work with one developer, the more leads they'll send your way for projects you don't need to negotiate commissions on.

Lender Relationships

The relationship with a lender, private or institutional, cannot be dismissed. A lender's job is to prequalify clients for loans. They also have people calling them on occasion who haven't even selected a home yet. These prospects are the type of people who shop after knowing their budget and also tend to be the better kind of client.

<u>This is an untapped mine for agents</u> who overlook the connection with lenders. What happens to the leads from lenders if they don't have a go-to agent to recommend? Agents should be prospecting lenders in their area and give them a personal visit. Don't just hand them a business card. Leave a mug with them as a reminder whenever they sip another cup of coffee while they're on the phone with these leads.

They're another valuable piece of the SOI puzzle. Offer them deals where they get referral commissions, and don't forget those crucial thank you notes. In fact, you can't send out enough thank you notes to your SOI crowd. Lenders are also synonymous for having bland lives outside of work according to daytime television. Take them for a beer to discuss your offer.

Taking Action

Setting up your lender relationships is easy because they need your contact for those phone calls. All you have to do is outshine the next agent in this relationship.

1. Make a list of every lender in your area. You can get this from company profiles if you work for a team, or you can Google it.

2. Visit one lender a day to introduce yourself as the new face of reality in your chosen niche.
3. Plan and host an event where you can invite the lenders to network with each other and yourself. This could be a competitive evening where you divide them into sports teams and offer a prize to the winner. Make sure you aren't the only person other than lenders, as that can be awkward. Invite some personal friends and contacts along, even tag team agents.
4. Keep in touch with your lenders at least once a month.

Pro Tip: The same rules apply to title agents and escrow officers. These are people you send business to all the time, and if you establish proper partnerships, they'll send business back. All you need, in most cases, is to ask.

CHAPTER 2:

Online Leads

Online lead generation can be a great supplemental strategy. There are so many options available, but they aren't all created equally. So, you need to know which online resources are credible, financially worthwhile, and add to your success. Your online success will depend on what type of leads you're looking for, and how much time you have to nurture them.

This chapter will focus on generating leads that fit into various intentions. I'll cover the most important types and give you an idea of how effective they are. Adding this supplement to your lead generation strategy can blow your business up if done the right way.

Expired and FSBO Leads

The first option we must delve into is the vast variations of online resources we can use to open our services to homes that are currently for sale by the owner and expired listings. New agents underestimate the impact they can have in FSBO leads because they think it's a brick wall; however, most of them have been at it for some time and are dying to ease the process.

Do it Yourself

Gathering potential leads by taking the long road can be profitable. The good news is that as long as you have access to a multiple listing service (MLS) database, you should have access to expired listings. Depending on which MLS you have, you might also have access to canceled or withdrawn listings. Canceled listings are a good target because they might've had a bad experience with their agents and need a trusted one.

The biggest problem you'll face on this database is to get the contact information for the expired listings, such as a name, contact number, or email. This would depend on whether the previous agent collected all this information or whether you have the right data. This can be a time-consuming and challenging task for agents. The solution to bypassing this is to look up the address in city and county records. This will help you find the contact information for the owner.

You simply need to visit your local town or county's public records official website. You can insert the address you have for the expired listing. Please take note that the owner's address might vary from the listing. This means you would need to add the owner's address to your database. Don't remove the listing address.

If you wish to find the owner's phone number, you can insert the name, address, and zip code from the public records into The White Pages (www.whitepages.com). This might bring up a contact number, but there are no guarantees. The reverse address feature on this platform could also bring results if you use the public records data.

Pro Tip: Be certain that the names you find on The White Pages match your expired listing as there may be a few results. A random wrong number could lead to a prospect in rare cases, but in most instances, it leads to awkwardness.

Expired and FSBOs Lead Generation Services: Address and Phone Numbers

Yes, agents should spend time scrubbing the MLS database, contacting other agents for leads on expired listings, and search public records for these gems. Still, there's a way of automating this information extraction from an MLS database.

This would be a paid-service that feeds expired listing contacts directly into your CRM, and all you have to do is follow up with them. This is optional if you have some money to spend on it.

Agents should take caution when they do this though. You still need to double-check that your expired and FSBOs aren't listed on the National do-not-call (DNC) list as this can get you into trouble with lawsuits.

Some homeowners and tenants will file a complaint against you if you skip this search. Fortunately, agents can check contacts on their national, state, or county DNC lists to make sure this doesn't happen. You can choose to go with a mail campaign or door knocking introduction instead.

There are two more important reminders here. Every MLS is different, and so are the rules of using them. You need to read the rules and regulations of each MLS before you start contacting expired and FSBO listings. Another reminder is that even paid lead generation websites will provide you with the listing address if the owner lives elsewhere. You'll have to do the public records research to make sure you have the owner's details.

Examples of lead generation services that specifically target expired and FSBO listings are LandVoice, RedX, Archagent, Vulcan 7, Mojo Autodialer, Metro Scan Search (MLS), Cole Realty Resources, and zBuyer. These service providers feed leads directly back to your CRM but come at a cost.

You can also use these two websites to search for more expired leads:

www.anywho.com/whitepages
www.searchpeoplefree.com

Using Google

The best expired leads are the fresh ones.

These can be found in the MLS hot sheets on various servers where there are quick property updates. The problem with finding expired leads is that these websites won't give you the contact numbers.

That's where the power of Google comes to the rescue. As the world's largest search engine, we can influence Google into giving us numbers if we know how to search for specific keywords. The bad news is that this sometimes works, and sometimes it doesn't.

There's always a silver lining in lead generation strategies. Using this method is excellent for new agents because it doesn't cost anything. This free method will be time-consuming, especially at scale. Teddy Smith, a marketing and real estate expert, gives us the formula for the lucrative Google trick (Smith, 2018).

All you need is the owner's name, address, and area dial code before you hit the search button. You can find the owner's name in the public records with the address. Now you click on the search bar in Google and type the owner's first and last name, followed by the address, and end it with the area dial code followed by an immediate hyphen. It will look something like this:

James Harrison 123 Broadway Road 999-

The hyphen that follows the area dial code is crucial to deceiving Google into giving you the information. The lucky results that return could be your sign to cold call these people. Just remember that Google numbers haven't been scrubbed for the DNC list yet, and you'll have to do this manually.

Expired Leads from Other Agents

I cannot emphasize enough the importance of having a network of partner agents. One more advantage of having this in your SOI is that you can share expired leads. You might even find expired listings in the portfolio of another agent who isn't at the brokerage anymore. You can contact these agents and offer them a deal. If you succeed at turning an expired listing back into an active one, you can offer them a shared commission.

Expired listings from other agents is a great strategy because there could be fewer agents on the job, giving you a higher chance of securing the listing. The owner thinks that all is lost when their listing expires, but they'll welcome a new face to the team with open arms in most cases.

The key is to start noticing previous agents' ledgers and sharing expired leads with your SOI network mutually through emails and social media. Another place to strike gold is by joining a specific social media groups where agents list their properties, discuss real estate, and share tips.

You can network online with Facebook, LinkedIn, Twitter, and various other platforms we'll cover in the next chapter. Always be on the lookout to exchange expired listings. Some properties don't do well with one agent, but a fresh face could get them sold. You can offer these group members a referral fee, and quickly expand your business.

Blogging for Leads

There's no doubt. Blogging is a goldmine for leads. Most agents think that blogging is outdated; that's precisely why you must take advantage of this.

I've discussed the figures: 84% of top agents and agents, have a website with a blog, post content, and engage with their clients weekly.

Commerce, retail, and any other form of sales, including real estate, move to the online world's frontlines. Our biggest source of leads is getting younger by the day, and these people use online platforms to connect with us.

New agents, in particular, can use their website as a gateway to direct engagement. So, I urge you once more to get a website up, and running. <u>It doesn't need an internet data exchange (IDX) with other agents from the start (if you have it awesome!).</u>

Your focus is on generating leads for yourself right now, and multiple listing services aren't a priority at first. You can always return to this when you've increased your SOI.

Your website must provide value, as this gives you the highest returns long term. You need a place where you can engage with your leads once a week while offering them valuable insights and current property news.

Potential leads can either see you as someone who just wants to make a killing in sales or see you as someone who wants to bring them the best experience. Blogs can quickly generate 10 to 50 leads a day when they mature. The secret here is to keep your blog active all the time.

The greatest part of having a blog is that this online presence keeps working for you while you're out there prospecting for business yourself. You can still cold call, door knock, and attend conferences while your blog acts as an automated salesman. Let your blog help you reach the top leagues of real estate agents.

Taking Action

1. Get a website with a blog where you can post content weekly. You can hire a web designer or use www.wix.com to create a simple one to start.
2. Start posting content from day one.
3. Do some research on Google keywords and SEO content.

4. Add something of value to every blog post. You can add market news or tips on decorating a home from a top designer.

Pro Tip: Have fun with your leads on your website by adding a hint of humor to your blogs.

Real Estate Website with Search Features

Expanding your business quickly can become very simple if you add IDX and search optimization features to your website.

Keep in mind that you want your website to add possibility and ease for clients. Your website visitors should be able to search properties listed, receive update notifications, and save favorites within your MLS. This means that any changes to a property, whether under contract or offer, will let people know who saved the listing as a favorite.

Updates should run every 15 minutes. Can you imagine that? We're living in an incredible of world possibility. Your potential leads will automatically get a notification just because they favorited a listing on your website.

Additionally, the ease of this design can allow your potential leads to find you faster and capture your contact information. There are also lead magnet pages and landing pages that could entice your leads to leave their information to contact them.

People don't save listings for no reason. The chances are that website visitors are people who actively participate in the market to buy or sell a property. They are motivated leads.

Taking Action

1. Contact a leading designer on agent websites, such as www.proagentwebsites.com.
2. Discuss lead generation options for desktop, mobile, and tablet formats.
3. This website should have a blog, landing page that acts as a lead magnet to capture client information, and the valuable CRM as you'll get busier over time.
4. Also, discuss live mapping with an integrated IDX search linked to an MLS.
5. It's best to add SEO content to reach a higher ranking on Google, and you can also involve Google Analytics to keep your ranking at the top of search pages.

Pro Tip: You should also consider adding social media pixels to your website code to bring Facebook followers to your website directly. The advantage of this is that these visitors are motivated and have fewer restrictions on capturing client information.

It also helps you with the social media costs if you choose to pay per conversion. For example, you could pay for a social media campaign that leads directly to someone clicking on "contact now."

Raffles and Giveaways

Who doesn't love receiving a gift or winning a prize?

This strategy could fit into your 33-point contact plan twice a year. I suggest you send out an email blast to your contact list before the holidays. This should include customers and real estate prospects where you can entice them to respond to a giveaway. This acts as a massive lead magnet for you because these people are more likely to remember you after receiving something for free.

They might even refer you to someone when they attend a party over the holidays and hear someone talking about selling a home. Suddenly, you pop into their minds after they won tickets to a Broadway show. I've gone over the advantages of referrals already. Referrals will become your number 1 seller if you make sure they happen.

Turning a raffle or giveaway into a purposeful referral program is also a great strategy. You can use email or direct mail to get people on your side with this one.

Taking Action

1. Choose a prize, not any prize. **A High-Value Prize**. When you do your research, you'll notice what your targeted audience value the most.
2. Decide how your entries will compete. You could ask contacts to help you build your contact list further. Each person gets an entry into the competition when you have a new lead's email, phone number, and names.
3. Set a date for when the competition ends.
4. Announce the winner on your blog.
5. Add a bonus thank you gift to anyone who has brought you a closing lead. Send them a bottle of champagne and a handwritten note. Also, announce this on your website.

Video Emails

Video emails are another holy grail of lead generation.

Statistics don't lie as Bomb Bomb surveyed to confirm what video emails can do for you. Video emails caused a significant increase in leads for 77% of participants, and 20% of them experienced <u>double their usual figures</u> (Beute, 2015). Over 80% of participants received more responses, 68.21% increased their conversions to motivated buyers, and 55.88% got more referrals.

<u>The click-through rate (CTR) was nearly **90%,**</u> and the participants who found the communication more effective were over 90%. These are high numbers that we can't dismiss. Many people will automatically delete a lead magnet email before they even read it, but people have always been more <u>inclined to watch a video instead</u>. Email campaigns can be grueling and leave us with little to no results if we lose lead interest.

Sending videos out will encourage our recipients to hear our message. It doesn't matter what the message conveys. It could be informative, breaking news in the real estate sector, or it can just be a follow up to see how a buyer is doing after they moved into their home. Conversions increase because more recipients actively hear your message, and the personalization of this method can skyrocket your referral network.

Taking Action

There are some key points to keep in mind with video emails.

1. Outline the message you want to send. Is it a lead magnet where you'll entice people with a special listing this coming weekend? It could also be a tutorial where you share some great tips for DIY projects.
2. Record a video on your laptop or use video email websites to help you, such as___ or activecampaign.com or www.mailchimp.com
3. Keep your video short, concise, and friendly. Long videos with excessive megabytes can cause your email to head straight to the spam folder.
4. Don't opt for an autoplay on these videos. You don't know where your viewer is sitting when they open it.
5. Use a hook in your subject line to make them open the email. Make it look personal and not aimed at 1,000 recipients.
6. Choose a call to action for the end of your video. Encourage people to visit your website, come to an open house, or ask you for advice on real estate.

"Google My Business"

It's simple yet profound. Most people are aware that Google is used in every corner of the world. You can now go into Google and browse coffee shops, restaurants, retailers, and even a pet grooming service nearby. It's an untapped market that many agents and agents overlook. They also ignore the benefits of reviews on Google.

Successful agents have claimed their spot on the Google map. They can be found, and millions can see their reviews of people. Google was one of the first to offer reviews so that people could make decisions based on what other clients have experienced. This is another powerful mechanism to sell yourself and generate leads that could turn into business without blinking an eye.

42 % of all businesses in the US have no presence on Google (Fox, 2019)!

This is tragic because 69% of home buyers start their search on Google.

Every business, no matter what kind, must be on Google. Any business or agent who forgets to claim their spot on the map allows people to review their services publicly and isn't doing their best to succeed. Don't let people create your story; take control.

Taking Action

Creating a Google Business presence is your official local SEO driver. Optimization of your setup is critical.

1. Start by setting up a **Google Business Account for free** when you visit www.google.com/business.
2. Be precise about your location, available hours, contact details, services offered, and add an about blurb.
3. Add your website to optimize the connection.
4. Add photos for people to see you and your real estate brand.
5. Add a video and some attributes if you have any.

Pro Tip: Keep an eye on your account and respond in a friendly, but professional manner to any reviews you receive. Your responses are also public.

Notice of Default Filings

A default filing happens when a public notice is filed with the court where a homeowner defaults on their mortgage.

The mortgager has failed the agreed terms and payments with the lender. The lender then goes off to court and files the paperwork. Lenders must provide the homeowner's names, contact information, physical address, default property's address, and why the mortgagor has defaulted.

A notice of default is the first step a lender takes to enforce foreclosure on a property.

This can be an emotional time for the homeowner because they might've defaulted for reasons beyond their control. Nevertheless, agents have a job to do, and many don't focus on the default filings for all the emotional attachment that comes with it. *These agents don't realize that they have two leads for every filing at their disposal.*

You can either target the lender or the homeowner who might need help selling their home after agreeing to do so. You can even target both parties. Whoever needs your assistance in selling the property is your best bet.

Lenders will be easier to persuade since they have no emotional ties to the deal. In most cases, the truth is that lenders and homeowners will prefer doing what's needed for both parties to get the most out of their original agreement. That's where you step in.

Taking Action

1. Having lenders on your SOI list is a great advantage, but if you don't, you can always

approach your local title companies that can provide a list of default filings in your area.

2. You can also look at larger companies that offer these lists, such as Norcon Marketing or Resource.
3. Record both lender and borrower's details like their names and contact details.
4. Understand the reasons behind the default before contacting anyone.
5. Contact the lender first and explain that you'll also be in touch with the borrower.

Remember to be sympathetic towards both parties as any defaulted contract often leaves both with invisible wounds.

Video Tours

Video tours provide an arsenal of benefits.

Research proves that people are 4 times more likely to engage with a video tour listing (Biteable, n.d.).

It's not only beneficial to buyers as 73% of homeowners prefer agents who give them the video tour, and only 9% of agents offer this!

This is a golden opportunity for you, knowing that buyers make decisions on visual stimuli more than the outdated wordy descriptions.

There's no better way to showcase a house or building than to walk through it and talk to your viewers as you do.

Taking Action

Let's learn how to prospect for buyers with a killer video. Don't forget to ask your seller if they'd like this option first.

1. Take the video viewer on a tour that tells a story of the home. Combine the power of storytelling and visual imagery.
2. Focus intently on the home features if there's a rolling lawn, fountain, or even a kitchen island that provides space and ease.
3. Pick the right time of day to capture the home in its best light as you notice the visual quality of the video.
4. Keep the video short but engaging.
5. Ask the seller if they'd like to answer questions about the home, which can be used as a brief 60-second interview at the end of the video.
6. You can also add community efforts to a video if this doesn't stretch the length too far. Let people talk about why the area is excellent for them. Potential buyers will love getting to know their future neighbors.
7. Add a call to action at the end of the video. I recommend that you show your face at the end to reach for brand awareness as well, and add a call to action.

Some agents live stream their videos from their website, Facebook, or YouTube.

At the beginning agents can perceive live streams as something uncomfortable to do, because there are a few things that are unpredictable during a live stream, but this is why it really sets you apart, it allows your audience to connect with you, and discover your personality in that moment, which creates empathy and affinity, leaving a more profound impression on them. They want to know that you're a real person.

The last part of creating video tours is to decide where you're distributing them. Many brokerage websites, agents websites, and MLS services have a video upload option. You can go with this, or you can turn your attention to YouTube.

Pro Tip: To create a compelling and effective video tour for your listing there are a few key elements that will allow you to stand out:

- A great question could be : "How do you conduct a public open house, without having the public there? You can use <u>Zoom.com</u> and in the setting section <u>make sure</u> to create a registration before the live, so you can automatically capture their info and reach back to them.
- Your video should be about 4 to 6 minutes max. Studies have shown that short videos are the best. The shorter the video, the more people will keep watching.
- Many agents don't leverage their offer by describing what it might be like to live in the same neighborhood. Take advantage of your environment.

YouTube Videos

This is extremely important to notice: *Many people don't know that YouTube is also a* **search engine***, much like Google. It isn't a social media platform*.

Google and YouTube also offer a double whammy as your videos are more likely to rank on the partner search engine before articles do. Google is integrating YouTube videos into their search results to get on the visual stimulation train.

Best of all is that YouTube is user friendly. It's great for new agents to gain some attention.

People don't mind watching amateurs on video rather than slick professionals who inevitably have ulterior motives. YouTube also doesn't require professional photography and expensive equipment. It just needs an agent who focuses on bringing something engaging and valuable to their viewers.

Taking Action

Allow your potential leads to engage with a real person rather than a block of words on an article or listing. There a few key points to keep in mind when you create a YouTube video.

1. Create your YouTube account with a personal email.
2. Highlight your brand and personality in your videos. Don't hide on the wrong side of the camera.
3. Define a clear outcome for your video. It doesn't need to sell a house. It could be an introduction to

the highlights of an area or designer tips from a local interior guru.

4. Create a hook in your video title. Put your name in there, so people remember you, such as "James Harrison takes you deep into the heart of a mysterious home."
5. Always use a brief introduction in each video. Not everyone knows you yet, especially if you're new.
6. Be a positive face who always smiles broadly. Friendliness is attractive and more approachable.
7. Be consistent in your visual branding in your video. Stick to the same color themes, lengths, and the call to action that comes last.

Pro Tip: Many agents get a basic website from their brokerage.

I recommend that you spend some money and amp up your own website. It doesn't matter if you have a detailed MLS at your brokerage or a blog.

What happens when you switch brokerages?

You'll lose all the information you have. The same applies to a brokerage email. You should use an email from your website to link to YouTube and any other lead platforms. Think long term, or you could lose all your efforts a few months down the line.

CHAPTER 3:

Social Media

Social Media is already widely accepted as a branding tool for agents, but it can also be a powerful lead generation tool. The best agents use social media as an extension of themselves to reach more clients and capitalize competitively. Social media offers us further connections with our clients and supports real estate marketing efforts.

According to studies conducted by NAR, social media has become integral to scoring clients and closing deals (National Associations of Agents Research Group, 2018). Some results showed that 77% of agents actively use social media in some shape or form to promote themselves. 47% of brokers noticed that social media brought more quality leads than other types of strategies.

This report also shows that 99% of millennials and 90% of baby boomers begin their home search online. The overall usage of social media in real estate amounts to 97% for Facebook and 59% for LinkedIn. This shows that nearly every agent uses social media.

Let's see how you can gain more leads with this opportunity or step up your social media game.

Facebook FSBO Groups

Facebook is one of the most powerful platform for real estate lead generation because so many people have access to it.

Some agents don't realize that Facebook has millions of active users who can be a potential lead at any given moment. Facebook also offers a marketplace, and it's not just a social platform anymore. People buy and sell in their local area. This interface works similarly to Google mapping, where users can look for products close to them.

An agent can gain more qualified leads through Facebook by joining relevant groups.

Numerous groups in your area are dedicated to FSBO listings. You can jump onboard these groups, and post some enticing information to attract attention. Besides real estate groups, you can also broaden your horizons with industry-relevant groups. You can join home improvement, landscaping, garage sale, and small business networking groups.

Taking Action

1. Setting up a Facebook page for yourself is where you start.
2. Make sure your page is brand relevant while adding some character to it.
3. Pages should be updated at least three times a week with posts, videos, photos, and some form of engagement.
4. Start joining groups and other pages to interact with them.

5. Try to aim for three new group additions daily for the first month.
6. Participate in the groups by **giving value first** and posting relevant news, updates on the property industry, and engaging blog articles or videos.
7. Post a link back to your website or Facebook page on these groups.
8. **Share valuable information.** Be positively active and share tips and advice from famous designers, landscapers, and even an accomplishment by a local school.

Facebook groups are lead magnets as long as you have a capture or landing page in place. This is primarily a great source for seller leads.

Facebook Messenger Ads

The next element from Facebook is messenger ads.

These offer convenience and keep a potential client interested longer when they don't need to fill out mountains of paperwork. Messenger ads are a paid option, but they skip the part where clients must take 100 steps before giving you their information. Facebook users automatically fill out their contact details when they click on a messenger ad and then on "give permission."

These leads can open a live chat with you. Messenger ads also give us tools to set up automated responses for when we're not available. This is one more strategy that makes the possibility available to your leads.

Taking Action

The beauty with Facebook is that most of the paid marketing tools are easy to follow with captions that tell you what to do as you go along.

1. Set up an ads manager account from your page.
2. Create an ad from your page and choose your objectives to tell Facebook what your intentions for the ad are. Objectives are a vital part of paid advertising.
3. Choose how the ad is delivered.
4. Set a budget that aligns with how much you're prepared to pay per click (PPC). You can also choose to budget for specific actions, such as conversions to a landing page on your website.
5. Select your demographic audience and messenger format.
6. Keep an eye on the ad through the insights tab.

Facebook has built-in analytics that allows you to see how many people your ad reaches. Familiarize yourself with the insights menu so that you can see what works and what doesn't.

Facebook Referring Leads

There's another powerful tool hidden inside of Facebook. You can increase your referral network with other agents across the country. There are even groups where agents connect with out of town agents and share their leads.

Social media makes this simpler for us where we don't have to attend every conference or networking event across the country.

Taking Action

This lead generation strategy is easy once you know how to search for groups. Now all you need is to learn more about keywords. Click on the search bar at the top of your Facebook page, and type in words to look for these networking groups. These are your keywords because Facebook is another form of search engine. Now you can toggle between searching for groups, people, pages, and so forth.

Keywords you want to try are:

- Agents, brokers, or brokerages
- Real estate referral networks
- Real estate lead shares
- Agent portal
- Agentnetworking
- Top real estate agents

You need to add a town, state, or county name to your keywords, or you'll automatically get the same results all the time, or you'll be stuck with local results only.

Facebook Promote Rewards for Referrals

We've learned that many people will refer to someone they know, but only a small percentage of those people will remember to refer to you if they don't know you personally.

That's why your SOI only works on people who know you personally. However, you can improve these chances with your social media followers too. All you need to do is something that makes them want to refer you.

Many of your followers are prepared to share a referral when they're prompted to do so. You can't expect people to remember your name unless you give them a reason to. Similar to the email giveaways, you can set the same system up on your Facebook page. Incentives are a strong motivator for people. An agent who makes their followers know precisely what rewards they could get beyond the referrals they hope for... are the successful ones.

Taking Action

Reward your followers by setting up a Facebook rewards program. Organic followers can partake, and you can use a Facebook boost to get your post in front of more viewers. It's another paid promotional item, but it's worth it in the end.

1. Create a monthly post on your page where you provide a reward for the most referrals logged from it.
2. Boost this post to increase your traffic.
3. Each referral gets one entry into a draw.
4. Invite someone from the page to actively do the draw.
5. Choose a prize that's brand relevant, such as a home décor gift card or a free home valuation.

Facebook Mega Giveaway

Joe Soto, a real estate mogul, teaches us the value of using a mega giveaway to attract more than 1,000 leads without spending more than $100 (Soto, 2016). This is great news for new agents who don't have a huge budget yet.

A mega giveaway is a competition that gives away something of great value. It won't only generate leads, but it will also create brand awareness. Mega giveaways should be done once or twice a year, depending on your budget. You can even determine the best prize by creating a poll on your page to see what people want.

Some people might enjoy a video course, or an eBook relevant to real estate. Others will enjoy location guides, a housewarming party at your expense, or free adventure tours to see the local sights. The content you offer to your followers should be of premium quality and not the regular run-of-the-mill posts. You're about to run a paid competition, and you want people to take action, share your post, and be prepared to give you their information without thinking twice.

Taking Action

Once your goals and mega prize are in place, you can start creating a new Facebook ad.

1. Design a competition that provokes action, such as users sharing pics of renovations, home upgrades, or where they must show you their design skills.
2. Use www.canva.com to create a professional advert with all the sizes and requirements needed for an engaging Facebook ad.
3. Woobox is another paid software you can use. This one allows you to create an offer from their platform and is fully interactable with Facebook.
4. Open your ad with a hook heading again. You can say, "Share your home upgrades to win a trip for two to the home improvement expo in California."

5. Keep your ad copy text short. Both Woobox and Canva will guide you with the requirements.
6. Make sure your text is compelling enough to make people want to share it. Who wouldn't want a free weekend trip to California?
7. Add a relevant photo or carousel of pictures to the ad copy to make it visually compelling.

Pro Tip: Run a mega giveaway around the holidays. This makes the experience fun for you and your audience. You can ignite competition in followers by asking them to share photos of their decorated homes around Halloween and Christmas. Agents can also make their prizes relevant to the holiday itself, such as giving away sports tickets during the Super Bowl season.

Pinterest Seller Leads

Pinterest is highly underrated with agents. What many successful agents know is that we can use Pinterest to target an untapped source of leads.

Why do many people visit Pinterest? They're looking for visual ideas on how to decorate or improve their home. These people might not be on the buyer's list, but they are an endless source of sellers. Many Pinterest users are house flippers who buy a beaten home and turn it into a great find.

Agents can befriend these flippers so that they can sell their projects. In return, you can offer them leads or incentives. All agents need to create a lead magnet on their Pinterest by adding pins relevant to the entire industry, including designers and flippers.

Taking Action

1. Canva also has pin templates available for upload to Pinterest.
2. Choose your design and add something engaging. You can even add another contest or create a visual presentation to entice people to visit your website.
3. Download your image and add it to your Pinterest board.
4. Go into the board and click on the edit option.
5. Now you can add any landing page from your website. I recommend placing a landing page that relates to the pin and offers people a call-to-action. This could also be a blog post where designers who are potential partners could learn more about a new product or service.

Pro Tip: Create a visually compelling quote and pin it to your board. A quote will potentially ignite curiosity and send traffic your way. For example, "Home is where the soul of a designer lives."

LinkedIn Search

LinkedIn is the professional version of Facebook.

It's where people look for and find employment. This is what most people know, but they don't realize that it's far more than this. LinkedIn is also filled with groups where professionals can connect with others who have similar interests. This is where your targeted strategy comes in. *We can use LinkedIn to get in touch with expired and FSBO listings that have proven difficult otherwise.*

The reason contact through LinkedIn works is that it's considered a platform of professionals. Once you know how to connect with the people on this platform without having a mutual connection, you can bypass the email campaigns they don't trust. Your email will go via LinkedIn, and this will increase your chances of the recipient seeing it as authoritative and trustworthy. Therefore, LinkedIn can boost your response and conversion rates for your campaigns.

Taking Action

1. Search for a first and last name on Google, followed by the word 'LinkedIn' to get specific results.
2. Make sure you're focusing on the right name and surname. There might be a few results.
3. Bypass the inability to connect with the person by adding yourself to a mutual group. You can connect with them by browsing through the group members.
4. Associate your LinkedIn profile with your CRM to pick their contact details up through the platform and add it to your drip campaign list.
5. All that's left is to wait until they respond to one of your engaging emails.

LinkedIn emails

There is a feature that most agents don't use to their full advantage, and this is where many leads are lost.

LinkedIn sends every member an email once a week to show them who visited their profile.

Agents could use this to fish out buyers and sellers from a vast array of professional people once they see that they've visited their profiles. The person might've been considering property, and chances are that they have the money or motivation for it.

How can you get mass email notifications sent to potential leads to show them that an agent was interested in their profile?

There are many applications for that. One of which is called "LinkClump". It can quickly visit 400 profiles a day. It could bring you many professional leads with less to no efforts. "Snap Links Plus" is another useful alternative that can scoop up mass notifications.

Taking Action

Using LinkClump requires some guidance.

1. Add it to your Google Chrome browser as an extension. Chrome is necessary as it doesn't work with other browsers.
2. Go into your targeted LinkedIn group from Chrome.
3. Head to members and drag your mouse over the desired lot while holding down the shift key.
4. The extension will open all the pages instantaneously, so you might want to do it in batches.
5. Continue doing this with 10 groups every week.

Generating leads on social media is as simple as you see. Don't forget to be active by posting, sharing, boosting, and connecting with various platforms daily. You can even share pictures where you've been active in the community by volunteering at an animal shelter, or provide frequent updates for the local sports team you might sponsor when you have a bigger budget.

CHAPTER 4:

Print

The fact that the world has moved online leaves printed lead generation underrated and forgotten.

New agents must realize that print marketing is on the rise again because of the industry's dependence on technology.

Everyone's starting to use websites, Facebook pages, and email campaigns. All this is doing is creating a gap where we can capitalize on a forgotten piece of the puzzle.

People are more likely to notice a well-tailored direct mail than a standard email in an ocean of digital marketing. There are more agents online now than there were five years ago, which creates the ocean effect, or shall I call it a digital hurricane? How did agents succeed before the influx of technology?

They targeted people by door knocking and handing them business cards or printed material. Keep in mind that direct mail doesn't mean that you have to send it through the postal service. Walking up to someone's door and allowing them to meet the friendly face behind a piece of paper is a sure win. It could increase the efficacy of your direct mail campaign.

Nevertheless, print marketing is time-tested and proven to be reliable for agents. It's the last piece of the puzzle that you can use to give your prospects a personalized approach. Emails can be personalized, but recipients know well enough that they might be on a mailing list of 100 or more people. That piece of paper you drop in someone's mailbox or hand deliver to them is what makes a difference.

Find FSBO Leads in the Newspaper

Many new agents don't think about the homeowner who still relies on the printed newspaper.

Many people still love the crisp feel of newspapers between their fingers and don't rely on digital versions. These people are more than likely going to place their FSBO listings in their local newspapers. That's the first place you look for seller leads even if you think these people are adamant about hiding their listing from online agents' prying eyes.

The truth is that these homeowners have no idea how the cost of newspaper advertising can snowball, and after a few weeks, they realize it. Some serious advertisers can spend a few hundred dollars a week on classified ads to promote their home. Most of these homeowners will quickly realize that the ends don't support the means.

Besides the cost of classified advertising, they're also so limited to what they can do. They're limited to exposure for their property and don't have the value of video advertising. They also have to sift through their potential buyer leads themselves, which can be daunting for them. The first few weeks are a blitz of marketing their home, and gradually their enthusiasm dies down as the costs pile up. That's when you come in.

Taking Action

1. Buy your local newspapers every week.
2. Watch the classifieds and track the progress of homes that aren't selling.
3. Give the advertiser a week or two before you contact them.
4. Make sure you have a friendly demeanor as they'll be agitated from their misguided efforts.
5. The secret is to start devising a campaign strategy before you approach them. You must be able to tell them exactly how your campaign will get more eyes on their home than the lackluster efforts of the newspaper.

Mailers

Direct mail will never go out of fashion, just like business cards will never become obsolete.

Handing one to a prospect is a confirmation of the possibility that the two of you might do business in the future. Mailers don't work for every agent, but you could be the one who builds a full pipeline from it.

The Direct Mail Association explains that we can achieve a 3.7% house rate return and 1% prospect responses from a direct mail campaign (Total Expert Team, 2016).

The figures aren't high, but if you can turn one in every hundred deliveries into a single genuine lead, the campaign was worth it. Many agents are more than happy with the low percentage because it can hook one client that becomes part of their SOI and automatically brings more business over weeks, months, and years. Turning that one client into a silent salesman depends on how you deal with them. Mailers offer a customer service level that digital lead generation doesn't, and this could make one percent response rates viable.

Taking Action

Direct mail can become an incredible source of business if you do it right.

Title agents are where you start because they have a higher chance of entering your SOI if you keep working on your relationship.

1. Find a title agent who you'll work with. Be friendly and approachable from the start.
2. Pay them a personal visit and hand-deliver your business card, printed leaflets, and promotional brochures. Make sure all your contact details are clear.
3. Tell the agent that you're looking for an exclusive relationship with a title agent for that area. We should remain with the same title agent as the city they work in. It builds a stronger relationship in the long run.
4. Confirm the mutual benefits where you'll be sending leads their way as well.
5. Ask the title agent for a list of properties. They might sell it to you at first, but you'll notice that some will give it to you for free once you're passing leads to them.

Most cities are separated by numbers, and you can pick the areas you want to focus on to create attractive brand-specific mailers targeted to an area.

Send Letters to Absentee Owners

We must understand the difference between *drip* and *direct mail* before we continue.

Drip mail is the kind where you have 100 brochures designed for a general objective and send them out to random people on a mailing list. This isn't direct mail, even if it goes through the postal service.

Direct mail is where you target specific demographics and send them letters or brochures that relate to them personally. That's what we'll do with absentee owners because they make up a huge demographic.

Absentee owners could include anyone who rents their property out to tenants. They could be working abroad or living in another town. No need to explain to agents how challenging lease agreements are. I'm sure you manage a few yourself. These owners only need the right push to turn them from a landlord to a seller. Your letters target a specific group of absentee owners that will ignite a direct response from them.

These letters should also create top-of-mind awareness and branding for your real estate services. Some of your recipients might not have ideas about selling or find it challenging to do so because they're far away. It's your job to plant a seed in their minds and let it grow. You must be kind-hearted, well-reasoned, and show favorable appreciation conditions.

Taking Action

You're going to sell yourself to someone who wasn't fully aware that they needed you yet.

1. Find an area that's filled with tenants.
2. Use public records to get the owner's residential addresses for communication.
3. Create a letter that keeps the community, friendliness, and reason in mind.
4. Speak to the homeowner like a friend while remaining professional.
5. Collect data about home values, community lifestyle, and anything relevant to why they should consider selling their homes. Home values might be on the upward trajectory, which can be motivation enough if they have bad tenants. It's key to focus on favorable conditions for the potential seller.
6. End your letter with an introduction to who you are, your influence in the community, and a call to action to contact you if they'd like a digital meeting.

Send Personalized Outreach to Expired Listings

Expired listings are a hot target for many marketing strategies.

However, it's open season, and agents from all over the place will be swooping to get their piece of someone who has become disheartened. Agents aren't magicians, and we know this, but an expired listing homeowner has been disappointed by one before and needs someone they can trust to do their best.

Adding a personal touch to this process could make you stand out from all the vultures circling the seller. Many agents use templates and send uninspiring letters to these people.

These letters commonly speak of selling the property bluntly with no personality and are usually followed by a list of credentials.

Taking the time to send personalized letters to owners of expired listings significantly increases the likelihood of a successful prospect. It shows the owners that you're sincerely interested in helping them. If done correctly, sending personalized offers could be one of your top prospecting methods. Everyone you reach out to needs an agent. All you have to do is make them choose you.

Taking Action

1. Research everything you can about the property and the owners.
2. Look into previous marketing strategies.
3. Double-check the price before designing your letter.
4. Open your letter with a hook, such as "Your home deserves the right family."
5. Introduce yourself without too many credentials and fluff. The focus should remain on the homeowner and even the community. Be friendly and compassionate about their long journey.
6. Tell them about your chosen marketing strategy that you've personalized for their home. Add some statistics to show how well that strategy works.

7. Invite them for a light lunch or a cup of coffee to discuss their home further. Keep the meeting personal by avoiding the cold office.

Local Businesses and Relocation Leads

Local businesses also come up as a constant reminder that we need relationships with the companies around us.

Print marketing can be useful in this scenario too. All you need to do is approach businesses in your area and get into the human resources (HR) department. The HR department can tell you who handles incoming and outgoing executive relocations. For example, if you live in Silicon Valley, you'll have a long list of technology companies you can target.

Ask the HR director if you can place a printed brochure in the break room so that relocation executives can find the resources they need. This could bring you a mass of relocation leads. After all, these executives don't know the area or have no personal connections in most cases. Having easy access to your information could make relocation more pleasant for them.

Agents might work in a military town where you can target The United States of America Army (USAA) relocation networks to help soldiers settle their families. There are countless opportunities in this print market. It starts with a cold call to the companies where you speak to someone in charge of relocation. Then you can offer to drop off any printed material in person that would help the inbound and outbound relocation process become smoother.

Taking Action

1. Invite your prospect for a 20-minute meeting at a local coffee shop.
2. Ask them what you can do to make the relocation transitions less stressful for them.
3. Come prepared with any work you've done to show them you're capable. You might want to focus on the average types of homes you have listed that would suit certain demographics.
4. Remain friendly and reassuring that you know how difficult relocation is, and you can make it much easier.
5. Drop off the brochures you promised at their office the morning after your meeting. Leave some business cards, brochures, and a coffee mug with your brand if you have the budget.

Now you have five proven methods of using print marketing to generate more leads.

Pro Tip: Another form of print marketing that coincides with digital marketing is text messages. 98% of successful responses on an agent and homeowner communication (Campaign Monitor, 2019) happens at the beginning of the interaction. Once you have an initial connection with your clients, text messages are the middle ground between digital and print touchpoints.

CONCLUSION

We have so many agents in our country that it makes real estate one of the most competitive industries, especially for new agents who aren't known to anyone. Real estate requires us to build a network of people who trust us, and others who greet us in the streets when they remember who communicates with them regularly.

You want your face to be the one that pops into someone's mind when they hear a friend talking about selling their home. You want your name to get into every corner of your neighborhood. Applying these strategies outlined in this guide can change the game for you and build a robust pipeline for your business.

I shared with you methods that top brokers around the country use to generate massive leads, build their brand, team, and success. You can apply them and test combinations that will work for you in your context. All you need to do now is experiment and focus on a combination of techniques that consistently generates positive results.

Don't hesitate with any test run, no matter how hard it might seem at first. Lead generation will become an automated skill once you have your killer combination. It's time for you to enter the challenge now and show yourself what you're truly capable of.

THANK YOU

We've come to the end of this book. I want to say **thank you** for reading.

I have one quick favor to ask.

If you enjoyed it, I'd be grateful if you left a brief review about it on Amazon.

It'll take 60 seconds of your time.

I appreciate your feedback because it will genuinely make a difference, so people can learn about this book.

Warmly,
James

ABOUT

James Harrison is a career strategist, sales leader, and teacher at heart. For James, real estate is all about integrity and fairness.

With nearly 15 years of residential and commercial real estate, James collaborated with top-performing agents in the industry, including a two-year assignment running one of the biggest new agent broker training programs in California.

He has also created multiple products to help agents and investors start building an incredible future. James has a tremendous talent for taking people brand new to real estate and transforming them into market leaders.

James's mission is to help people achieve extraordinary results in life and sales through personal and professional development.

Today, he dedicates his time to support his associates by providing them cutting edge training and coaching.

REFERENCES

Adams, B. E. (2018, September 29). *The 6 types of real estate leads for agents (and which is best)*. Hooquest. https://hooquest.com/types-of-real-estate-leads/

Ad Espresso. (2019, August 5). *4 Smart ways to attract more real estate leads with Facebook*. Ad Espresso by Hootsuite. https://adespresso.com/blog/real-estate-leads-with-facebook/

Beute, E. (2015, October 2). *Survey: 77% of people benefit from video email, 20% double results.* Bomb Bomb. https://bombbomb.com/blog/video-email-survey-results-reply-response-referral/

Biteable. (n.d.). *Real estate video marketing for agents & estate agents*. Biteable. https://biteable.com/blog/real-estate-video-marketing-for-agents-estate-agents/

Campaign Monitor. (2019, January 18). *ROI showdown: SMS marketing vs. email marketing*. Campaign Monitor. www.campaignmonitor.com/blog/email-marketing/2019/01/roi-showdown-sms-marketing-vs-email-marketing/#:~:text=Research%20shows%20that%20SMS%20open,to%20respond%20to%20an%20email

CA Realty Training. (2017, June 26). *Ep. 35: What is a real estate agent's sphere of influence? | How to maximize your reach*. YouTube. www.youtube.com/watch?v=WvarXrEAQ3s

Clothier, K. (2018, May 11). *7 Types of leads real estate pros need to know about.* Real Estate Worldwide. https://reww.com/blog/7-types-of-leads-real-estate-pros-need-to-know-about/

Davidson Realty Incorporated. (n.d.). *Davidson referral network.* Davidson Realty Incorporated. www.davidsonrealtyinc.com/team/davidson-referral-network

Easy Agent Pro. (n.d.). *Lure leads with these real estate giveaway ideas*. Easy Agent Pro. www.easyagentpro.com/blog/real-estate-giveaway-ideas-leads-website/

Easy Agent Pro. (2015, January 13). *How to get more Pinterest leads as a realtor.* YouTube. www.youtube.com/watch?v=NlJxd99cG7w&feature=emb_title

Esajian, J. D. (n.d.). *How to generate free real estate leads with a referral network.* Fortune Builders. www.fortunebuilders.com/free-real-estate-leads-referral-network/

Fox, J. (2019, May 8). *Is Google my business for real estate agents?* Jason Fox. www.jasonfox.me/is-google-my-business-for-real-estate-agents/

Gateless. (2016, February 29). *Don't ignore your past clients.* Gateless. https://gateless.com/articles/close-buyers/being-irreplaceable-after-the-sale

Gateless. (2016, February 29). *Stay top of mind post-close.* Gateless. https://gateless.com/articles/close-buyers/stay-top-of-mind-post-close

Gateless. (2016, February 29). *10 Powerful marketing touchpoints.* Gateless. https://gateless.com/articles/market-your-business/10-powerful-areas-of-potential-touch-points

Icenhower Coaching. (2016, December 6). *Develop a real estate agent referral network.* YouTube. www.youtube.com/watch?v=jrbjpGBQkmo

Kagan, J. (2020, June 20). *Notice of default.* Investopedia. www.investopedia.com/terms/n/notice-of-default.asp

Kailas, M. (2016, September 27). *5 Essential tips for networking in real estate.* Entrepreneur.com. www.entrepreneur.com/article/281743

L'Eplattenier, E. (2019, September 26). *How this Georgia agentgets 70% of her clients from YouTube.* The Close. https://theclose.com/get-clients-from-youtube/

McAllister, C. (2019, January 24). *Client touch points.* Roost Real Estate Company. https://roostrealestateco.com/client-touch-points/

Mimeo. (2015, May 4). *The do's and don'ts of real estate print marketing*. Mimeo. www.mimeo.com/blog/the-dos-and-donts-of-real-estate-print-marketing/

Montgomery, M. (n.d.). *8 x 8 Real estate touch ideas for agents*. Rev Real Estate School. www.revrealestateschool.com/tips/8-by-8-real-estate-touch

National Association of Agents Research Group. (2018). *Real estate in a digital age: 2018 Report*. National Association of Agents. www.nar.realtor/sites/default/files/documents/2018-real-estate-in-a-digital-world-12-12-2018.pdf

Patel, N. (n.d.). *How to include video in your email marketing*. Neil Patel. https://neilpatel.com/blog/video-email-marketing/

Real Estate Trainer. (2016, December 8). *Build a real estate agent referral network*. The Real Estate Trainer. https://therealestatetrainer.com/2016/12/08/real-estate-agent-referral-network/

Resendiz, J. (2019, October 1). *Real estate lead generation Facebook Ads - How to get more real estate leads in 2020*. YouTube. www.youtube.com/watch?v=o_5v8tcai9g

Rudden, J. (2020, January 6) *Number of National Association of Agents members in the United States from 2009 to 2019*. Statista. www.statista.com/statistics/196269/us-national-association-of-agents-number-of-members-since-1910/

Rudden, J. (2020, May 13) *Number of housing units in the United States from 1975 to 2019*. Statista. www.statista.com/statistics/240267/number-of-housing-units-in-the-united-states/

Simmons, Q. (2020, March 5). *Home buying desires of millennials mirror silent generation, agentreport finds*. The National Association of Agents. www.nar.realtor/newsroom/home-buying-desires-of-millennials-mirror-silent-generation-realtor-report-finds

Simmons, Q. (2019, November 7). *Families using creativity when buying, selling homes: 2019 Buyer and seller survey*. The National Association of Agents. www.nar.realtor/newsroom/families-using-creativity-when-buying-selling-homes-2019-buyer-and-seller-survey

Smith, T. (2018, February 12). *Where to find FSBO, expired, and cold-calling leads (FREE)*. YouTube. www.youtube.com/watch?v=b3wAz763otk

Sopielnikow, C. (n.d.). *How to build a real estate investment network like a pro*. Fortune Builders. www.fortunebuilders.com/build-a-real-estate-network/

Soto, J. (2016). *How to collect 1,000 emails in 72 hours with less than $100 in Facebook advertising*. https://drive.google.com/file/d/1kry4Bp-XF2G7-uWFJJ7ATaV8bPP81Yk_/view

Total Expert Team. (2016, February 18). *Don't overlook the value of real estate print marketing*. Total Expert. https://blog.totalexpert.com/real-estate-print-marketing

Westlund, R. (2020, March 27). *8 Places to find global referrals & 8 more referral networks to consider*. Florida Agents. www.floridaagents.org/news-media/news-articles/2020/03/8-places-find-global-referrals-8-more-referral-networks-consider

Zey, T. (2019, June 11). *53 Ways to generate real estate leads with 1 secret that will blow your mind!* Easy Agent Pro. www.easyagentpro.com/blog/generate-real-estate-leads/

Zey, T. (2019, June 11). *6 Little known ways to get seller leads as a realtor*. Easy Agent Pro. www.easyagentpro.com/blog/6-little-known-ways-to-get-seller-leads-for-free-as-a-realtor/

Zey, T. (n.d.). *How to get started in real estate (with a Bang!) – The ultimate guide for starting your sales career*. Easy Agent Pro. www.easyagentpro.com/blog/how-to-get-started-in-real-estate/

Zey, T. (n.d.). *Use this little known Facebook feature to generate free real estate leads [Takes 3 Minutes, Scripts Included]*. Easy Agent Pro. www.easyagentpro.com/blog/free-real-estate-leads-on-facebook/